THE
Living World

ANN FULLICK

Heinemann
LIBRARY

First published in Great Britain by Heinemann Library,
Halley Court, Jordan Hill, Oxford OX2 8EJ,
a division of Reed Educational and Professional Publishing Ltd.

Heinemann is a registered trademark of Reed Educational & Professional
Publishing Limited.

OXFORD MELBOURNE AUCKLAND
IBADAN JOHANNESBURG GABORONE BLANTYRE
PORTSMOUTH (NH) USA CHICAGO

Designed by AMR
Illustrations by Art Construction
Printed in Hong Kong

02 01 00 99 98
10 9 8 7 6 5 4 3 2 1

ISBN 0 431 07626 X

British Library Cataloguing in Publication Data
Fullick, Ann
The living world. – (Science topics)
1. Biology – Juvenile literature
I. Title
570

Acknowledgements
The Publishers would like to thank the following for permission to reproduce photographs:
Heather Angel pg 4; Jacana pg 28; Peter Gould pg 16; Planet Earth Pictures pgs 7, 10, 12, 14,
25, /Adam Jones pg 19, /Paul Harcourt Davies pg 20, /Margaret Welby pg 29 top right, /John
Bracegirdle pg 29 bottom right; Science Photo Library pg 8, /NASA pg 5, /Adam Hart-Davis
pg 13, /B. Murton/Southampton Oceanography Centre pg 17, /Dr Yorgos Nikas pg 22;
Southern Newspapers plc pg 24.

Cover photograph reproduced with permission of Bruce Coleman Limited/ Michael Fogden.
Cover shows ants on a leaf over a background image of a leaf.

Our thanks to Geoff Pettengell for his help in the preparation of this edition.

Every effort has been made to contact copyright holders of any material reproduced in this
book. Any omissions will be rectified in subsequent printings if notice is given to the
Publisher.

Any words appearing in the text in bold, **like this**, are explained in the Glossary.

Contents

The seven signs of life

The study of living things is called biology. While the millions of living organisms in the world appear to be very different, they do have some things in common. There are seven characteristics of life that take place in all living things – they feed, respire, move, **reproduce**, excrete, grow and are **sensitive** to the world around them. If we can show that something has all of these characteristics, we can be pretty certain it is alive.

Moving, growing and sensitivity

It should be easy to see things move – but it is not always. The movements of large **animals** are usually quite easy to spot, but those of very small animals and **plants** can be almost invisible to the naked eye. It is also difficult to see things growing. Growing means developing existing **cells** and making new cells. Most living organisms grow slowly and some take years to get big enough for us to notice the change.

It is often important for animals or plants to move or grow in one direction rather than another, so all living organisms have some way of being sensitive to the world around.

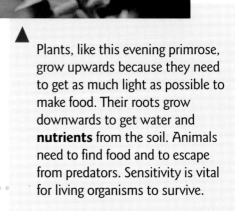

▲ Plants, like this evening primrose, grow upwards because they need to get as much light as possible to make food. Their roots grow downwards to get water and **nutrients** from the soil. Animals need to find food and to escape from predators. Sensitivity is vital for living organisms to survive.

Feeding, respiring and excreting

All living things need energy to move, grow and reproduce. They get their energy from food. Plants can make their own food using a process called **photosynthesis**. Other organisms have to take in food by eating plants or animals.

Much of the food taken in is used to supply energy to the body. Energy is released from the food in a process known as **respiration**. As organisms use their food, they make waste products. Getting rid of these waste products is known as **excretion**.

Reproduction

All kinds of living things can reproduce to make young just like themselves. It could be said that everything living organisms do is designed to make it possible for them to reproduce. If organisms do not produce offspring, then that type of organism will soon die out. Living organisms use all sorts of ingenious methods to make more of themselves.

Life on Mars?

Space exploration took on a new dimension recently when rock fragments from a meteorite were found to contain what looked like **fossils** of **bacteria**. The origin of the rock was thought to be the planet Mars – and if these really are fossils then it means that at some point in time there has been life on another planet in our own Solar System. Scientists are carrying out lots of tests to see if they can find evidence to show whether these 'fossils' were ever really living, or whether they are just unusual patterns in the rock.

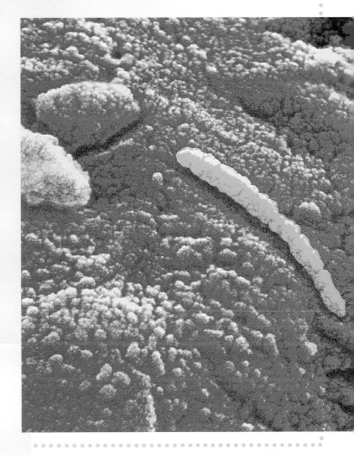

▶ The meteorite in this picture is thought to have come from Mars. The tube-like structure (which has been coloured blue) may be a fossil bacterium – evidence that there was once life on Mars? It is less than 1/100th the diameter of a human hair.

The five kingdoms

The living world contains millions of different types of living organisms. We organize them into groups to try to help us understand more about them.

What is a plant?

We probably all have a mental picture of a plant as being something green with leaves and possibly flowers or fruits. But to be scientific about it, we must find features all plants share. First and foremost, plants can make their own food by **photosynthesis** using water and carbon dioxide.

The energy they need to do this comes from sunlight, absorbed by the **chlorophyll** found in the leaves and stem of the plant. This is known as **autotrophic nutrition**. Secondly, plants respond very slowly to their surroundings by gradually moving only one part of their body.

PLANT CELL

ANIMAL CELL

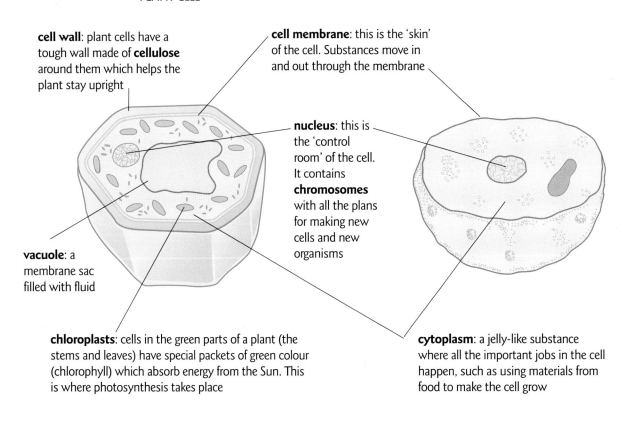

cell wall: plant cells have a tough wall made of **cellulose** around them which helps the plant stay upright

cell membrane: this is the 'skin' of the cell. Substances move in and out through the membrane

nucleus: this is the 'control room' of the cell. It contains **chromosomes** with all the plans for making new cells and new organisms

vacuole: a membrane sac filled with fluid

chloroplasts: cells in the green parts of a plant (the stems and leaves) have special packets of green colour (chlorophyll) which absorb energy from the Sun. This is where photosynthesis takes place

cytoplasm: a jelly-like substance where all the important jobs in the cell happen, such as using materials from food to make the cell grow

There are times when it is difficult to decide whether a living organism is an animal or a plant. But if we look at animal and plant **cells** there are a number of clear and distinct differences, particularly if we choose cells from the green parts of the plant.

What is an animal?

Our mental picture of an animal is doubtless very different from that of a plant. Animals tend to be very active, moving their whole bodies or parts of them very quickly and responding rapidly to changes in their surroundings. Also, animals cannot make their own food. To obtain the energy they need, animals (such as humans) must take in food by eating other organisms. This is known as **heterotrophic nutrition**. Some animals eat plants, some eat animals, some eat a mixture of the two.

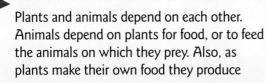

Plants and animals depend on each other. Animals depend on plants for food, or to feed the animals on which they prey. Also, as plants make their own food they produce oxygen which animals need to **respire**. Plants need animals to fertilize the soil, and to help them **reproduce**. Animals also produce the carbon dioxide plants need to make food.

The five kingdoms

Although the two largest groups of organisms in the living world are the animals and the plants, there are actually five kingdoms altogether. This is because there are some organisms that simply cannot be described as either animals or plants.

The **fungi** are probably the best known of the other groups – things like yeasts and toadstools that don't move their whole bodies, but which cannot make their own food. They are all parasites or **saprophytes**, digesting either living or dead organisms to supply themselves with food.

The **prokaryotes** (**bacteria**) are probably the oldest kingdom – it is thought that life on Earth began with simple cells like these. Some bacteria cause disease, but many others are important for maintaining a healthy body or for recycling many **nutrients** in nature.

The **protoctists** (mainly single-celled organisms like protozoa) live mostly in water or within the bodies of other living organisms. Some can make their own food by photosynthesis, others cannot. They make up most of the plankton in the oceans and seas.

Cells, cells, cells!

Some living organisms are made up of a single cell, others consist of billions of cells. Every cell is an amazing miniature chemical factory, producing the **molecules** needed for life to exist.

SCIENCE ESSENTIALS

Cells are the tiny building blocks of life. Cells that do particular jobs are different from 'typical' **plant** and **animal** cells – they are adapted to the job they do.

Seeing is believing

To see most cells we need to use a microscope. We have learnt a great deal about cells using light microscopes which were developed in the 17th century. But the detail we can see is limited by the wavelength of light. Over the last 50 years our knowledge of the inside workings of cells has been greatly increased by the development of the **electron microscope**, which uses a beam of electrons instead of light to form the image. When you use a light microscope you usually magnify your specimens a few hundred times at most. The electron microscope allows us a magnification of up to 500,000 times!

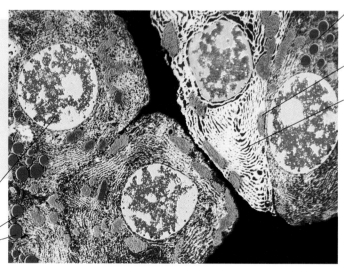

This is a picture of cells from the pancreas taken using an electron microscope. The cells have been magnified 1,200 times and are specially coloured so you can see the different features.

cytoplasm

mitochondria

folded membranes covered with ribosomes which are producing the digestive enzymes

cell **nucleus**

packets full of **enzymes** ready to go to the small intestine

A world of their own

Many organisms consist of a single cell which carries out all the functions of life. In larger organisms the hundreds, millions or billions of cells also operate almost like minute individual organisms.

They obtain energy from food by **respiration**, they get rid of waste by **excretion**, and they **reproduce**, making new cells to replace old ones, for growth and for repairing damaged tissues.

An assortment of cells

In every cell a large number of chemical reactions are taking place in a very controlled way. Keeping all of these reactions working at the right speed without interfering with each other is the job of the cell enzymes. In large **multi-cellular** animals and plants many of the cells are adapted for highly specialized jobs. They often work together as tissues or organs to carry out these jobs – examples include the eye, a leaf, the liver, the skin and a flower. Animal cells in similar tissues (such as eyes, muscles, livers) tend to be quite similar even if they are in different animals, but they generally differ clearly from plant cells. When we look in detail at some of these cells we can see how they are adapted for their particular functions.

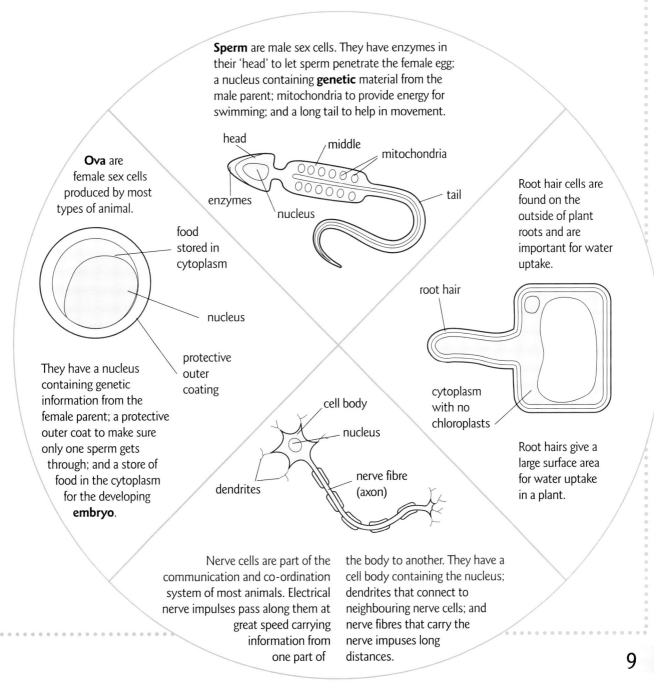

Sperm are male sex cells. They have enzymes in their 'head' to let sperm penetrate the female egg; a nucleus containing **genetic** material from the male parent; mitochondria to provide energy for swimming; and a long tail to help in movement.

head
middle
mitochondria
enzymes
tail
nucleus

Ova are female sex cells produced by most types of animal.

food stored in cytoplasm

nucleus

protective outer coating

They have a nucleus containing genetic information from the female parent; a protective outer coat to make sure only one sperm gets through; and a store of food in the cytoplasm for the developing **embryo**.

Root hair cells are found on the outside of plant roots and are important for water uptake.

root hair

cytoplasm with no chloroplasts

Root hairs give a large surface area for water uptake in a plant.

cell body
nucleus
nerve fibre (axon)
dendrites

Nerve cells are part of the communication and co-ordination system of most animals. Electrical nerve impulses pass along them at great speed carrying information from one part of the body to another. They have a cell body containing the nucleus; dendrites that connect to neighbouring nerve cells; and nerve fibres that carry the nerve impuses long distances.

Movement

The flight of a bird, the galloping of a horse, the slow response of the root of a **plant** to **gravity** – the movement of living organisms takes a wide variety of forms.

Movement in plants

When we think of plants, we don't usually think of them moving. But while plants do not move their whole bodies about, techniques such as time-lapse photography have shown that parts of plants are very active.

When a seed starts to grow, it may have fallen or been planted in the ground the wrong way up, yet roots always grow downwards – how? Plant root **cells** seem to be **sensitive** to gravity. This means that whichever direction a root is pointing when it first emerges from the seed, it moves and bends to grow towards the pull of gravity – downwards!

New shoots move away from gravity and then, when they break through the surface of the soil, they move towards the light. These movements are called **tropisms**.

Plants move on a daily basis too. Leaves move to follow the Sun across the sky, making sure that they are continually angled to absorb as much light as possible. Many flowers open in the daytime when insects are about and then close their petals as the light fades in the evening. So although plant movement is slow, it is nevertheless an important part of plant life.

Plant movement is not always slow! The 'trap' of the Venus fly trap snaps shut so quickly it can capture fast-flying insects such as this fly.

Animal movers

Movement is also important for **animals**. Animals move to catch or find food. Animals that may get eaten need to move to get away. If conditions in an area are unsuitable, animals move to a better environment. Movement matters for the very survival of the **species**, because many animals need to move around to find a mate if they are to **reproduce**.

Flying, gliding, floating, swimming, jet propulsion, moving on four legs, two legs, six legs or many legs – in animal movement almost anything goes. In **vertebrates**, movement is brought about by muscles pulling on bones. The same basic principles are behind the movements of animals as varied as fish and birds, people and crocodiles.

No bones – no movement?

There are far more **invertebrates** than there are vertebrates, but how do they move without bones? There are a number of different solutions to this problem. Many invertebrates, including insects and crustaceans (crabs and their relations), have a hard, strong skeleton on the outside of their bodies. Their muscles are attached to this **exoskeleton** and pull on it to cause movement. Other invertebrates, like worms and slugs, rely on **hydraulic skeletons**.

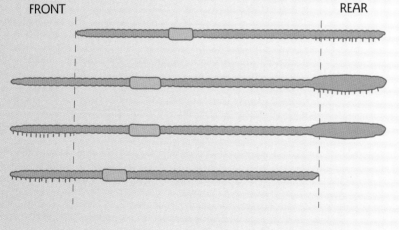

FRONT   REAR

Small bristles (chaetae) are extended to anchor the rear of the worm.

Circular muscles contract, squeezing the worm so it becomes long and thin and extending the front end.

Chaetae are withdrawn at the rear, and put out at the front end.

Longitudinal muscles contract to shorten the worm again, moving it forward.

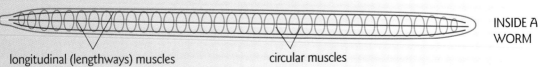

INSIDE A WORM

longitudinal (lengthways) muscles   circular muscles

▲ Animals with hydraulic skeletons, such as worms, have bodies that are tubes containing fluid which cannot escape. By using muscles to squeeze the tube and move the fluid about, all or part of the body can be made to move.

11

Plant feeding

Plants need an energy source just as much as any other living organism, but they don't eat food – they make it! The needs of a plant are small – provided they have plenty of water, air and sunlight they can make food in the process known as photosynthesis.

Food factories

The leaves are the food factory of the plant, because this is where photosynthesis takes place. To make sugars a plant needs carbon dioxide and water. Carbon dioxide (in the air) gets into the leaves through small holes or pores known as **stomata**. Water enters the plant through its roots and travels up the stem to the leaves.

When light energy hits the leaf it is trapped in the **molecules** of the green pigment **chlorophyll**, which is contained in small bundles called **chloroplasts**. The energy is used to join carbon dioxide and water molecules together to form sugar molecules, making oxygen as a waste product. This oxygen passes out from the leaf through the stomata. Getting rid of waste products like this is known as **excretion**.

The sugar formed in photosynthesis is quickly built up into starch molecules. This starch is then transported around the plant and carried to all the individual **cells** in the veins. In the cells it may be used for storage or converted back to sugar for **respiration** or growth.

It is amazing to think that all of the plant material in this vast Peruvian rainforest was formed from carbon dioxide gas in the air, and water from the soil, using energy from the Sun.

The first plants

Back in the mists of time when life was first evolving on Earth, it seems that there was little or no oxygen in the Earth's **atmosphere**. The only organisms that could survive were **bacteria**-like cells which did not need oxygen for respiration. It was not until the arrival of the earliest plant cells, carrying out photosynthesis, that the levels of oxygen in the atmosphere began to rise. As plants became more and more successful, oxygen levels increased until it was possible for **animal** cells, depending on oxygen for respiration, to **evolve**. On Earth today we remain dependent on plants to maintain oxygen levels in the air and to prevent levels of carbon dioxide from getting too high.

The root of the matter

Photosynthesis takes place in the leaves of the plant to produce carbohydrates, but plants also need to make proteins and fats. To do this they need other chemicals which they get in the form of minerals, taken into the plant through the roots. Below the soil surface, the network of roots holds the plant firmly in the soil. They also take up the water needed for photosynthesis. Dissolved in the soil water are many minerals which are moved actively (using energy) into the plant by the root hair cells. This makes sure the minerals are carried into the plant where they are used to make many important molecules – including chlorophyll itself.

SCIENCE ESSENTIALS

The roots of a plant hold it firmly in the soil, and take up water and other substances that the plant needs to grow. Minerals such as nitrates, phosphates and potassium are also important for plant health.

When we give our house plants 'plant food' or spread fertilizer on our fields, we are making sure that the plants do not run out of minerals they need.

▶ In this photo you can see the parts of a pea plant above and below the soil. The green, chlorophyll-containing leaves carry out photosynthesis and provide the basic food for the plant. The roots provide the water needed for photosynthesis and supply the minerals needed to convert basic food molecules into a wide variety of plant material.

Animal feeding

Like plants, animals need a source of energy and of building materials for their bodies. But unlike plants, animals cannot make their own food – they have to find it and eat it!

Plant-eaters

Plants make their own food. They are enormously successful and grow in vast numbers all over the surface of the Earth, both on land and in water. It is not surprising, therefore, that many different types of animals feed themselves by eating plants.

Plant-eaters are known as **herbivores** and they include many different types of organisms.

All of the largest land animals are plant eaters – elephants, rhinos, zebras, giraffes – yet many tiny **invertebrate** organisms are herbivores too.

The big problem facing herbivores is that it is very difficult to extract the nutrition they need from plant material. Each **cell** is encased in a **cellulose** box (the **cell wall**). Animals do not make the enzyme **cellulase** needed to break down cellulose. So when plant material is eaten, a lot of effort must go into breaking open the cells so the contents can be digested. Plant-eaters have flat, ridged teeth and spend a long time chewing, smashing and grinding open the cells. Many of them also have very large, long and often complicated guts so that as much digestion as possible can take place. Some animals, such as cows and termites, have **micro-organisms** living in their guts which make the enzyme cellulase, allowing the breakdown of cellulose. But one common feature of all herbivores is that there is always a lot of undigested food passed out of their bodies.

Animal-eaters

Animals that eat other animals are called **carnivores**. There are usually many herbivores available to eat – the meat-eaters just have to catch them. If herbivores run away to avoid being eaten, carnivores need to make sure that they do not use more energy chasing their prey than they will finally get from eating it.

Some carnivores eat smaller carnivores whilst others simply scavenge – they only eat animals that are already dead. Animals are relatively easy to digest as their bodies are made largely of protein and fat, so carnivore guts are usually quite short and relatively few pieces of solid waste (faeces) are produced.

▼

Carnivores have **evolved** a range of different strategies to enable them to capture and eat their prey.

Sea anemones have stinging cells on their tentacles to paralyse their prey.

A bit of both

Some types of animals, including humans, eat a wide range of food that includes both plant and animal materials – they are known as **omnivores**.

Camouflage means that a chameleon is not noticed by its prey until it is too late.

A plague of plant-eaters

Some herbivores can have a devastating effect on human life. Locusts, for example, form vast swarms containing millions of insects. Wherever they land they eat every bit of plant material, destroying crops and grazing over huge areas. Attacks by plant-eaters such as these have caused thousands of people to starve – and we still fight to control them today.

Respiration – energy for living

Plants make their own food, animals eat food and the food is a store of energy. To get at that energy, living things use a special set of chemical reactions known as respiration.

SCIENCE ESSENTIALS

Respiration in cells involves the reaction of glucose and oxygen to give energy that the cell can use, and carbon dioxide and water as waste products. Respiration takes place in the mitochondria of the cells of all living things.

Energy for everything

The human body has systems to make sure that plenty of food and oxygen reach the cells. The digestive system breaks down the food we eat into small, soluble molecules such as glucose.

Our respiratory system breathes air into our bodies and gets oxygen into our lungs. Our circulatory system transports food and oxygen to our cells. What do they do with it all?

Lots of different reactions take place in your body, such as repairing damaged cells, making new cells and producing the great variety of chemicals needed for your body to work properly. All of these reactions need energy. Respiration takes place in cells to make the energy from your food available for your body. The same reactions take place in the cells of almost every kind of living thing.

When glucose and oxygen react together they form carbon dioxide and water, and lots of energy is released, as you can see! In an uncontrolled reaction like this, the energy is in the form of light, heat and sound. In the body, the reaction is carefully controlled to make usable packets of energy for the cell.

The powerhouse of the cell

Within the **cytoplasm** of almost every cell are tiny **organelles** called mitochondria. Inside each mitochondrion is a mass of folded membranes. Sited on these membranes are the **enzymes** that carry out respiration, allowing oxygen and glucose to react together in a carefully controlled way.

The energy that is produced is in the form of a special chemical, **ATP**, which can easily be used to supply energy to other cell reactions that need it. The waste products water and carbon dioxide move out of the mitochondria to be excreted by the cell and then eventually by the whole organism.

Black smokers

Some recently discovered organisms seem to defy all our normal expectations of living things. Cells usually die at temperatures over about 40°C because their enzymes are made of protein which is damaged by the heat.

'Black smoker' **bacteria** live in deep vents almost 3,000 metres below the surface of the sea. The pressure is enormous – enough to crush most life forms – and the temperature coming up from the core of the Earth is around 350°C. In fact, if it drops below 100°C (the boiling point of water) 'black smokers' cannot **reproduce**. No-one yet understands the biology of these remarkable bacteria.

◄ 'Black smoker' bacteria live in this vent deep in the ocean. Mineral-rich fluid is pouring from the vent's mound, which is 18 metres high.

Waste disposal

Living organisms produce lots of waste from the reactions that take place inside their **cells**. What happens to it all? Much of this waste is poisonous and would kill the living organism that produced it if it were allowed to build up.

Common waste

All living things respire, and during **respiration** they produce carbon dioxide and water as waste products. Water is no problem – it is needed in both **plant** and **animal** cells. Any excess passes out of the cells of a simple animal or plant. It moves out of the **stomata** in the leaves of a **multi-cellular** plant, or moves out in the exhaled air of a more complex animal. Carbon dioxide is different. In plants, the carbon dioxide that is produced by respiration is largely used up to make more sugars during **photosynthesis**. Any that is not used passes out through the stomata. For animals the carbon dioxide is poisonous and so it must be removed as quickly as possible. In some animals it is removed in the air that is breathed out. In fact, it is often the levels of carbon dioxide in the blood that control the rate of breathing. This is because if carbon dioxide builds up, the breathing rate increases to get rid of it.

Human excretion

Human beings, in common with other animals, have to eat food to get energy. The problem is that when the food is broken down during digestion, and as the food **molecules** are used up in the body, chemicals are produced that we do not need – and which are poisonous to our bodies. The most important of these is urea, formed when proteins are broken down. In humans the organs that deal with the removal of urea from the body are the kidneys – the excretory organs. Most other multi-cellular animals have excretory organs to deal with their own protein breakdown products. As adults, people also get rid of waste through their sweat, but the solid waste (faeces) which we all pass out of our bodies at regular intervals is not true excretion at all. It is not the waste products from chemical reactions in our cells – it is simply the food material that we cannot digest.

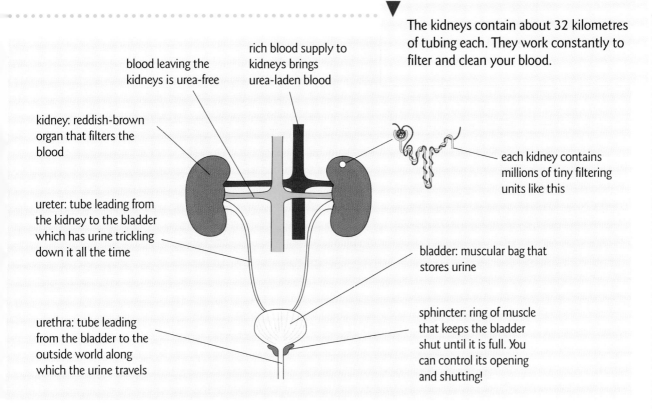

The kidneys contain about 32 kilometres of tubing each. They work constantly to filter and clean your blood.

kidney: reddish-brown organ that filters the blood

blood leaving the kidneys is urea-free

rich blood supply to kidneys brings urea-laden blood

each kidney contains millions of tiny filtering units like this

ureter: tube leading from the kidney to the bladder which has urine trickling down it all the time

bladder: muscular bag that stores urine

urethra: tube leading from the bladder to the outside world along which the urine travels

sphincter: ring of muscle that keeps the bladder shut until it is full. You can control its opening and shutting!

Plant excretion

Plants produce carbon dioxide and water as waste products of respiration. They also produce oxygen as a waste product of photosynthesis, and this passes out through the stomata of the leaves. But plants also produce other waste products, particularly if they are **deciduous** and their **chlorophyll** starts to break down in the autumn. All waste products are moved to the leaves and stored there in an inactive form that does not affect other reactions in the plant. Then there is a spectacular massive excretion each year when the leaves fall.

For evergreen trees (which keep their leaves all year round) the removal of this waste is gradual – each time a leaf falls a little bit of successful excretion occurs.

▶ These trees in North Carolina, USA, show excretion at its very best! The spectacular colours of autumn are the result of a build-up of waste products in the leaves, which are all removed from the tree when the leaves finally fall for the winter.

19

Reproduction in plants

Because no single organism lives forever, all living things need to reproduce if their **species** is to survive. The ways and means by which **reproduction** is successfully achieved vary enormously.

More of the same

Many **plants** reproduce asexually – they **clone** themselves. There are lots of different ways of doing this. Asexual reproduction is relatively risk-free for plants because offspring are guaranteed, even if they are always identical. We encourage plants to reproduce asexually whenever we take cuttings or graft new stems onto root stocks.

Runners (stems that grow out from the base of a plant on which new identical plants form), stolons (parts of normal stems that form roots and then new shoots wherever they touch the ground), and underground stems known as rhizomes (which develop new roots and stems at intervals along them) are all methods of asexual reproduction used by plants.

The same but different

When plants reproduce sexually they produce more of the same type of plant, but the new plants are not identical to their parents. Special sex cells, ovules (female) and pollen (male) meet and fuse to produce a new, **genetically** unique individual. The **embryo** plant forms within a seed. Ideally the sex cells come from two different plants, but even if they are from the same plant, the offspring will show more variety than if it had been cloned.

▶ Flowers contain the sex organs of plants – something to remember next time you see a display like this.

The male parts of the flower are the anthers which produce the male sex cells called **pollen**.

stigma

anther

ovary

style

ovules

TYPICAL FLOWER

The female sex cells, or ovules, are contained in an ovary and are reached through the stigma and style.

Plants rely on a variety of vectors (carriers) to carry the pollen from one flower to another. Many, like the grasses, have small, insignificant flowers and rely on the wind to carry huge amounts of pollen.

Other flowers rely on insects. They may have bright colours, distinctive patterns, strong scents and/or sugary nectar to attract insects to feed from the flower and to pick up pollen.

Plants produce sex organs containing special sex cells only when they need them. Pollen from one plant lands on the stigma of another plant (**pollination**) and travels down the style into the ovary, where the pollen **nucleus** can fuse with the ovule nucleus to bring about **fertilization**.

Once the ovules have been fertilized they develop into seeds, each one containing an embryo plant with a food store to supply the seedling as it starts to grow.

The ovary around the seeds – and sometimes other bits of the flower as well – form a fruit to protect the seeds.

If seeds fall straight under the parent plant they are unlikely to survive, because the seedlings will be competing with their parent for resources.

Exploding pod

Edible fruit containing seeds

Floating seeds

So they need to be spread away from the parent plant. This is known as **dispersal**. The fruits are often vital in this process – and may be adapted in all sorts of ways to spread the seeds as far as possible.

The ultimate sacrifice?

Within the plant **kingdom** there are many strange ways of dispersing seeds. One of the strangest is the tumbleweed of the American West. The plant has flowers and produces fruit. Then to disperse the seed the whole plant dies, to be uprooted by the strong winds blowing across the plains. The plants then 'tumble', rolling over and over, scattering their seeds as they go.

Reproduction in animals

Animals have the same need to reproduce as **plants** do. But because they can usually move around, their approach is often rather different.

Ovum + sperm = success

Successful fertilization that results in the development of a new individual is the aim of all sexual reproduction. Animals use a wide range of methods to try to make sure that this happens. The methods vary depending on the type of animal and whether it lives on land or in water. Getting the eggs and sperm together may be left to chance with aquatic animals because the sex cells can survive in water. However many species have courtships which make the meeting of gametes more likely. But animals that live on land must transfer the sperm from the male directly into the body of the female, as the delicate gametes cannot survive in the air.

After successful fertilization, the developing offspring and the young may also need care. There are two main reproductive strategies. The first is to have lots of offspring and let them manage alone, gambling that at least a few will survive. The second is to produce relatively few offspring, but invest a lot of time and effort in making sure they survive.

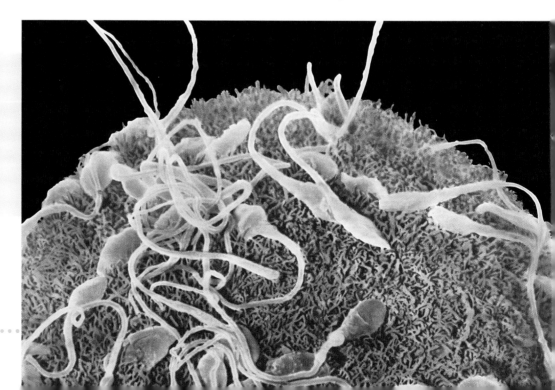

The moment of fertilization, when a human egg and sperm meet, marks the beginning of a new individual.

Some fish, amphibians and molluscs have developed very complicated courtships to make sure the sperm and ova are positioned as closely together as possible in the water.

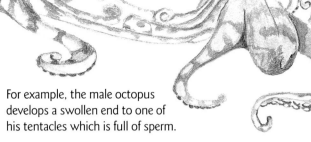

Small animals living in water, such as hydra, produce sex organs seasonally and release vast numbers of sex cells into the surrounding water.

For example, the male octopus develops a swollen end to one of his tentacles which is full of sperm.

After courtship, he gives this 'sperm pod' to the female who places it inside her body to fertilize the eggs before they are laid. She then guards the eggs, looking after them until they hatch.

It is then a matter of chance if those gametes meet with others from a different animal and fuse successfully. The gamble usually pays off and the **species** have no problems surviving!

After mammals mate, the embryo develops inside the uterus of the mother. It is provided with warmth, food and oxygen until it is born. Some mammals are quite independent at birth, whilst others are still very helpless. Whatever they are like, the mother feeds them herself on milk from special mammary glands.

Reptiles, like these tortoises, lay eggs with leathery shells which hatch when the young are fully formed.

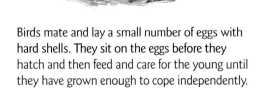

Mating is not always easy to accomplish! And once the ovum and sperm have joined successfully in the body of the female, the embryo must be protected as it develops.

Birds mate and lay a small number of eggs with hard shells. They sit on the eggs before they hatch and then feed and care for the young until they have grown enough to cope independently.

Animals use all sorts of different methods, but they all manage to reproduce.

Making sense of the living world

People have always wanted to create order out of the seeming chaos of living things and classification helps us do this.

Why classify?

As travel has become increasingly common and communications have improved, it has become easier for scientists and thinkers across the world to talk to each other and exchange ideas. From the mid-18th century it became increasingly important that everyone called living organisms by the same name. When a Swedish botanist, Carl Linnaeus, wrote his *Systema Naturae*, carefully classifying many of the plants and animals known at the time, the book had an instant audience.

The binomial system

The system Linnaeus worked out has lasted so long mainly because it is still useful. He used Latin, the universal language of scholars at the time, so his system worked across language barriers. Also he gave all living things a name made up of two Latin words – the binomial system of naming. The first term shows the **genus** to which the organism belongs. The second term shows the species of the organism – a species is a specific group of very closely related organisms within a genus, and it identifies organisms exactly. Members of a species can breed together and produce fertile offspring. Animals that are not of the same species but are very similar, like a horse and a donkey, may be able to mate and produce offspring. However, the offspring, in this case a mule, will be infertile.

► Don't judge by appearances! These two animals are members of the same species and can – if they overcome their physical difficulties – breed to produce offspring!

Look very carefully...

In the time of Linnaeus, the classification of living things was carried out entirely on the physical appearance of the organism. Today, we have a much more complicated classification system with many more layers.

There are also more complicated ways of deciding where an animal or plant belongs. We look at the outside of the organism but we also look inside, at how it develops as an **embryo** and even at the chemicals that make up its **cells**.

Human relations

It is easy for us humans to see ourselves as something unique and different from the rest of the animal **kingdom**. If we use a classification system based on external observation only, we may still convince ourselves that our superficial similarities to the apes mean less than our ability to wear clothes, drive cars and write books.

But when it comes to deciding species and their relationships using biochemistry – by looking at some of the most important **molecules** in the cells – the picture changes.

When we examine **DNA** (from **chromosomes**), haemoglobin from the blood and the **enzyme** cytochrome C, the differences between human beings and chimpanzees are very tiny indeed. Our cytochrome C is identical, our haemoglobin is only a few building blocks different, and we even have most of our DNA in common.

▼

Humans are very closely related to chimpanzees, and to some of the other apes. We are separate species – but only just!

Classifying animals and plants

About 2 million **species** of organisms have been discovered and described, but biologists think there may be ten times that number as yet unknown! On these two pages you can see the main groups of **plants** and **animals**, each with its own characteristics explained.

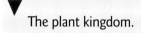

The plant kingdom.

spore

Ferns are much bigger than mosses. They have strong stems, roots and leaves. As their leaves are waterproof they don't lose much water. They have transport systems for water, so they don't have to live in damp places. Ferns **reproduce** using spores instead of seeds.

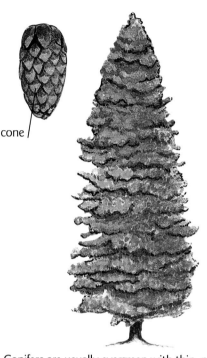

cone

Conifers are usually evergreen with thin, needle-like leaves. They have waterproof leaves and a water transport system. They produce seeds that are formed inside cones.

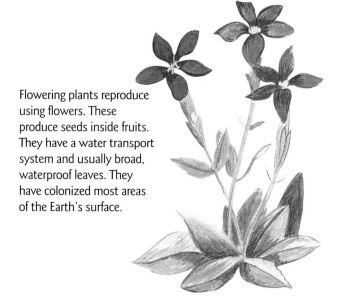

Flowering plants reproduce using flowers. These produce seeds inside fruits. They have a water transport system and usually broad, waterproof leaves. They have colonized most areas of the Earth's surface.

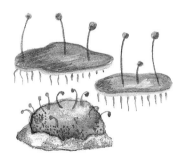

Mosses and liverworts are small plants that live in damp places because they lose water easily through their thin leaves and don't have a water transport system in their body. They reproduce making spores instead of seeds.

Birds have wings and feathers, and most of them can fly. They have beaks and lay eggs with hard shells. They often care for their young.

Reptiles have dry scaly skin and breathe air using lungs. They lay leathery-shelled eggs on dry land.

Mammals have hairy skin and can sweat. The young develop inside the mother's body and are born developed. The mother makes milk in her mammary glands to feed them.

Arthropods have jointed legs and a hard outside skeleton. This is an enormous group that includes insects (all with six legs), spiders, crustaceans, centipedes and millipedes.

Amphibians have smooth, moist skin. They can breathe through their lungs in air and through their skin in water.

They lay eggs in water.

Molluscs have muscular bodies. Most have a shell inside or outside their bodies and they are found in water and on land.

Segmented worms have long bodies divided into segments and breathe through their skin in air or water.

Jellyfish have jelly-like bags for bodies and tentacles to catch their food.

Flatworms have simple flat bodies.

They breathe through their skin in water or in air.

Fish live in water. They have gills for breathing, fins for swimming and scales on their bodies.

VERTEBRATES

INVERTEBRATES

ANIMALS

Roundworms have thin, smooth, rounded bodies and breathe through their skin in air or water.

Echinoderms have star-shaped bodies and live in water.

The survival of the fittest!

Where have all the **species** of organisms alive on Earth today come from? We can never know for certain, but by building up a picture from all the evidence we have available, we can get a good idea.

Time travelling

We cannot go back in time to see what the world looked like millions of years ago. But we can travel back in our imaginations as we piece together some of the evidence of life long ago. Some of the most important evidence we have comes from **fossils**.

A fossil is created when a living organism dies and becomes buried in mud or sand. The soft parts of the **animal** or **plant** will often rot away without trace, but the harder parts – stems, bones, teeth and shells – may be preserved and very gradually turn into stone.

When identifying a fossil we can compare characteristics of related living organisms, like the front limbs of mammals. Although they are adapted to do lots of different things, they all have the same basic pattern, which suggests they have a common ancestor.

The study of biochemistry can show us which living organisms have chemical **molecules** in common. This gives us more evidence about when groups of organisms became separate. But however much evidence we put together, we can never be absolutely sure that we have got it right!

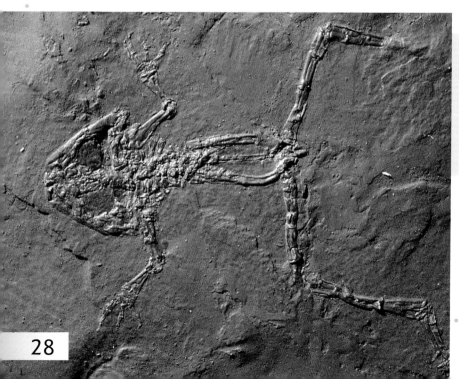

When we discover fossils they are often in pieces. It is like making up a giant and complicated jigsaw to discover what the organism was once like.

Evolution – survival of the fittest

Fossils found all over the world show us that living things have gradually changed over millions of years. Some kinds have become extinct (died out completely) and new kinds have developed to take the place of older ones. This process of slow change over millions of years is known as evolution. How does it come about? The members of any species differ slightly from each other and these differences may be passed from parents to their offspring. Members of a species also compete with each other for food and other resources. If one of the differences gives an organism an advantage, then individuals with that characteristic will tend to succeed in producing the most offspring. As a result, the species gradually becomes better adapted to its way of life and less well-adapted individuals die out. In this way the species evolves. This is known as survival of the fittest – the animals or plants best suited to their environment survive best. The first people to arrive at the idea of evolution to explain the variety of life on Earth were the biologists Charles Darwin and Alfred Russell Wallace, who lived and worked in the mid-19th century.

Filling a niche

Around the world there are many cases of similar habitats offering the same food supplies. Often these niches are filled with a wide variety of very different species – for example grass-eaters include small insects and horses! But sometimes a food source is so specialized that organisms which evolve quite independently in different parts of the world end up looking very similar. Nectar-rich flowers in four different parts of the world have resulted in the evolution of four different nectar-eating birds. But although they are from quite different species they are all very similar in size and appearance, particularly their beaks. This sort of evolution, where the same solution to a problem is adopted by widely separated species, is know as convergent evolution.

▲ The purple honeycreeper from Trinidad and the greater doublecollard sunbird from South Africa have evolved to fit similar niches in very different parts of the world.

Glossary

animal   a living organism that cannot make its own food and has to eat other living organisms for survival

asexual reproduction   production of offspring identical to their single parent

atmosphere   the blanket of gases that surrounds some planets. The Earth has an atmosphere of air

ATP   adenosine triphosphate, the main molecule that stores energy in a form which can easily be used by **cells**

autotrophic nutrition   making your own food

bacteria   micro-organisms that can cause disease

carnivores   animals that eat only other animals

cell   small, simple building block of any living thing

cell membrane   'skin' of the cell that controls the substances coming in and out

cellulase   **enzyme** needed to break down **cellulose**

cellulose   complex carbohydrate that makes up plant **cell walls**

cell wall   tough **cellulose** layer found around all plant **cells**

chlorophyll   green pigment found in plants that absorbs the energy from the Sun

chloroplasts   packets of the green colour **chlorophyll** where **photosynthesis** takes place

chromosomes   thread-like structures found within the **nucleus** of **cells**

classification   grouping living organisms by their similarities and differences

clone   organism reproduced by **asexual reproduction**

cytoplasm   jelly-like substance where many of the important reactions take place in a **cell**

deciduous   plants that lose their leaves in winter

dispersal   the spreading of fruit and the seeds they contain away from the parent plant

DNA   deoxyribose nucleic acid, the material of inheritance

electron microscope   microscope that uses a beam of electrons to form an image, giving high levels of magnification

embryo   a developing offspring

enzymes   protein **molecules** that change the rate of reactions without being affected in the process

evolution   the process of slow change in living organisms over long periods of time as those best fitted to survive breed successfully

excretion   getting rid of the waste products made by **cells**

exoskeleton   the hard external skeleton found in **invertebrates** such as insects and crustaceans

fertilization   the joining of a male and female **gamete** in **sexual reproduction**

fossil   the remains of an animal or plant that has been buried underground and has turned to rock over millions of years

fungi   kingdom of organisms that do not move around and cannot **photosynthesize**

gamete   sex cell

genetic   to do with genes, the units that pass on characteristics from parent to offspring

genus   a group of similar organisms

gravity   force that attracts all objects to each other. Plant roots grow towards the pull of gravity

herbivores   animals that eat only plants

heterotrophic nutrition   eating other organisms to provide food

hydraulic skeleton   skeleton based on fluid enclosed in the body and moved under pressure by muscles

invertebrates   animals without bony skeletons inside their bodies

kingdoms   the name given to the five different groups of living organisms

micro-organism   a microscopic living thing

mitochondria   found in the **cytoplasm** of cells, where the reactions of **respiration** take place, providing energy for the **cell**

molecules   the tiny units that can take part in chemical changes

multi-cellular   many celled

nucleus   the 'control room' of the cell, containing the **chromosomes**

nutrient   any food that gives nourishment

omnivores   animals that eat other animals and plants

organelles   small structures found inside **cells** that carry out particular functions

ovum/ova   female **gamete** in animals

photosynthesis   process by which plants make their own food using carbon dioxide, water and the energy from sunlight absorbed by **chlorophyll** in the **chloroplasts**

plant   living organism that makes its own food by **photosynthesis** and responds to its surroundings by moving parts of its body very slowly

pollination   transfer of pollen from the male organs of one plant to the female organs of another

prokaryotes   kingdom of organisms which include **bacteria**

protoctists   kingdom of organisms that are mainly single-celled

reproduction   producing new individuals of the same type of organism

respiration   the controlled release of energy from food using oxygen

saprophytes   organisms that feed on dead organisms

sensitivity   awareness of surroundings/the world around

sexual reproduction   involves the joining of special male and female sex **cells** to form an individual that is different from both its parents

species   specific group of very closely related organisms whose members can breed successfully to produce fertile offspring

sperm   male **gamete** in animals

stomata   small holes (pores) in the leaves of a plant that can be opened and closed

survival of the fittest   the theory that the animals or plants best suited to their environment survive best

tropisms   plant movements in response to a stimulus such as light or **gravity**

vacuole   fluid filled space in a **cell**

vertebrates   animals with bony skeletons inside their bodies

Index

28/5/09